THE 2004
INDIAN OCEAN
TSUNAMI

Essential Events

THE 2004
INDIAN OCEAN
TSUNAMI

BY MARCIA AMIDON LUSTED

Content Consultant
Thorne Lay
Professor of Earth and Planetary Sciences
University of California Santa Cruz

ABDO
Publishing Company

CREDITS

Published by ABDO Publishing Company, 8000 West 78th Street, Edina, Minnesota 55439. Copyright © 2008 by Abdo Consulting Group, Inc. International copyrights reserved in all countries. No part of this book may be reproduced in any form without written permission from the publisher. The Essential Library™ is a trademark and logo of ABDO Publishing Company.

Printed in the United States.

Editor: Karen Latchana Kenney
Copy Editor: Paula Lewis
Interior Design and Production: Rebecca Daum
Cover Design: Rebecca Daum

Library of Congress Cataloging-in-Publication Data
Lüsted, Marcia Amidon.
  The 2004 Indian Ocean Tsunami / Marcia Amidon Lüsted.
      p. cm. — (Essential events)
  Includes bibliographical references.
  ISBN 978-1-60453-047-6
  1. Indian Ocean Tsunami, 2004—Juvenile literature. 2.
Tsunamis—Indian Ocean—Juvenile literature. I. Title.

  GC221.5.L87 2008
  909'.098240831—dc22

                                        2007031214

TABLE OF CONTENTS

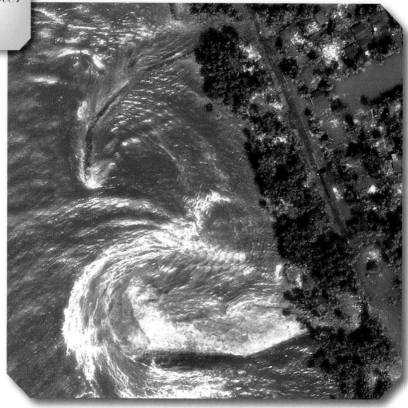

A satellite photo of the coastline of Sri Lanka shortly after the tsunami's impact

SWEPT AWAY

It was December 26, 2004. At a resort hotel on the west coast of Phuket Island in Thailand, tourists enjoyed the sunshine and the bright blue water. This area had become a new vacation destination for visitors from all over the world and was home to many luxurious resort hotels. On this peaceful Sunday afternoon, the sky was cloudless and serene. It looked like a vacation advertisement for a tropical paradise.

In the city of Banda Aceh, on the Indonesian island of Sumatra, most people felt the tremors of an earthquake in the Indian Ocean. Some of the poorly constructed buildings in the area trembled precariously or even collapsed, but the sea was calm. Most fishermen continued to go out in their boats as usual.

In Sri Lanka, an island off the coast of India, the early morning train, named The Queen of the Sea, that runs between the cities of Colombo and Galle was leaving the station. It was more crowded than usual because of a Buddhist holiday. Many people were visiting relatives and enjoying a day off. One thousand six-hundred passengers were crowded into eight passenger carriages. Many were hanging off the sides of the train as it headed down the west coast of the island.

On the beach at Phuket, tourists watched in curiosity as the sea surged out and away from the beach, leaving a wide strip of sand, rocks, and stranded fish exposed. Scuba divers suddenly found themselves standing or sitting on bare sand where they had been swimming only moments before. In some locations, the usual brilliant blue color of the water had changed. The ocean was now white and frothy. In some places it was a dark, oily black.

As people rushed down to the beach for a closer look at this amazing phenomenon, a giant wave suddenly came crashing onto the beach. Witnesses say the wave was at least 15 to 20 feet (5 to 6 m) high. The water swept over the beach and pushed onto the land. It carried with it people, furniture, and pieces of buildings. A woman from Canada recalled,

The water just smashed everything in its path. It came up over the beach, over the road running along the beach front, behind the main part of the hotel, and swept away large four-wheel-drive-vehicles.[1]

Further north along the coast, in the village of Nam Khem, a local woman named Watcharee sat on the front steps of her home with her daughters.

How Many Tourists?

It is estimated that 9,000 tourists were among those dead or missing as a result of the tsunami. Of all the countries with citizens who were vacationing in Indonesia, Sweden was the hardest hit with 428 dead and 116 missing.

She heard people screaming that a gigantic wave was coming and headed toward the beach to see what was happening. Author Erich Krauss wrote about her experience in his book *Wave of Destruction*:

> She made it only halfway. ... There was a massive wave coming straight at shore. It wasn't far off, perhaps 500 yards. ... Maybe it would break into pieces the moment it hit the shore, just like other waves. But this wave, instead of shrinking as it approached, grew in height. Soon it was as tall as a two-story building. Watcharee realized that the shore would not stop this wave. It would crash into the pier and then carry straight over the land.[2]

In Banda Aceh, a tourist riding the ferry between the city and a nearby island noticed that the ship bounced just a bit. Another passenger pointed to the shore and yelled "Tsunami!" The tourist saw that the wave's spray was moving back toward the ferry instead of heading toward the shore. It would be several hours, however, before the ferry landed and the tourists were able to see the full extent of what had occurred.

A Wall of Water

One of the most menacing things about a tsunami is the way that the ocean water moves. Normal ocean waves are created by the wind and only move on the surface of the water. With a tsunami, however, the entire ocean is moving from top to bottom. This creates a high, solid wall of water that hits the coast all at once.

Tourists watch as tsunami waves hit the shore outside a resort.

In Sri Lanka, the train stopped for a signal. Suddenly, a wave approximately 20 feet (6 m) high swept through the trees and pushed the carriages off the rails. Soon the railway carriages were tossed around by the waves and flooded with water, trapping and drowning most of those inside.

The first wave was followed by more waves. British tourist Paul Ramsbottom said,

It happened in cycles. There would be a surge and then it would retreat and then there would be the next surge which was more violent and it went on like that. Then there was this one almighty surge. I mean literally this was the one which was picking up pickup trucks and motorcycles and throwing them around in front of us.[3]

THE TSUNAMI WAVES

These deadly waves, known as a tsunami, swept onto the coasts of Sri Lanka, India, Bangladesh, Thailand, Malaysia, Sumatra, and Indonesia, as well as countless smaller islands. Eventually, the waves would even reach Somalia and other locations on the coast of Africa. The tsunami occurred during one of the busiest tourist seasons. Resorts were filled with international vacationers spending the holidays on the area's beautiful beaches and enjoying the sun and the warm sea. The waves came with no warning, and there was very little time to react once the waves began to strike land. The net result was the greatest loss of life ever caused by a tsunami, and one of the greatest natural disasters in human history.

Unlike the Pacific Ocean, the Indian Ocean rarely has tsunamis. Most of the tourists and residents who experienced this tsunami had never encountered one before. Catastrophic storms, such as hurricanes or tornadoes, usually give some warning of impending danger. Unlike those storms, the tsunami gave no indication that a disaster was about to occur. Curious tourists and natives who went toward the beaches to see the exposed ocean floor were unable to escape the sudden onslaught of the waves.

The tsunami waves repeatedly surged and retreated, leaving chaos and devastation behind them. The ocean waves carried debris more than one mile (1.6 km) inland from the coast. Household goods and appliances, fishing boats, cars, and pieces of buildings were all moved by the waves. Isnie Rizal, a driver in the town of Banda Aceh in Indonesia, said,

> I turned around to see the water coming into the city from two directions. The waves looked empty but on top they were carrying everything from cars to the roofs of houses. [4]

Many of the people swept up in the waves were crushed to death or seriously injured by the debris. Many also drowned when they were pinned underneath the water and could not get to the surface to breathe. Some were swept back out to sea when the waves retreated and their bodies were never found. Even fishermen out on the ocean died when the crests of the waves crushed their boats and swept them into the water.

Entire villages and resorts were destroyed or washed away. Millions of people were left homeless. Many of the local residents were poor and lived in homes that were not constructed to withstand such fierce waves. Their homes crumbled upon impact. What was left behind was covered in mud, seawater, large pieces of debris, and the dead bodies of the tsunami's victims. Low-lying areas were covered in flood waters that remained after the tsunami's waves had receded.

Local and Distant Tsunamis

Tsunamis travel at different speeds depending on the depth of the water they are traveling in. A distant tsunami travels away from its source across the deep ocean. It only forms a small hump of water that is spread over a broad region in deep water. But, the wave travels very fast, often between 300 to 600 miles per hour (483 to 966 km/h). A local tsunami wave moves toward the shore from a nearby source. As it moves, it slows to speeds of only tens of miles per hour. This forces the waves to become higher and steeper and hit the shoreline with a massive amount of energy. Local tsunamis may strike the shore within minutes after an earthquake, so there is little opportunity to give warning. Distant tsunamis may take hours to cross an ocean basin, providing an opportunity for people to anticipate its arrival if a warning system is operating.

Dirty Water

One of the greatest hazards of the tsunami came from the water. It was contaminated with dirt and hundreds of other bacteria from sewage and animal waste. These contaminants were picked up by the waves as they rushed over land. Those who survived the tsunami with relatively minor cuts or injuries often developed raging infections because of contact with the contaminated water. Those who inhaled the filthy water often developed pneumonia and other lung infections.

News of the 2004 Indian Ocean tsunami appeared on televisions across the world, as word of the disaster spread. Soon, images of the massive waves hitting the shore, captured by a tourist's video camera or cell phone, would become familiar. But even with the extensive media coverage, the scope of the tsunami would go well beyond the first images of the disaster. It would destroy the families, homes, and livelihoods of thousands of people.

As the morning of December 26, 2004, dawned, no one was aware of the trigger for the death and destruction that was occurring deep under the ocean, in the crust of the earth. One small shift, in geological terms, was going to result in one of the biggest catastrophes in human history.

A survivor amid the destruction caused by the tsunami in Sri Lanka

The third tsunami wave hits the beach in Ao Nang, Thailand.

A Seismic Bump

Tsunamis do not appear in the ocean without reason. Often, tsunamis are confused with tidal waves. Tidal waves are large waves formed by the interaction of the ocean's natural tides with the forces of the sun, the moon, or wind. The word *tsunami* means "harbor wave" in Japanese. It is the product of a disturbance that suddenly displaces a large quantity of water in the ocean. This is just like dropping a rock into a puddle, creating a ring of waves that travels outward from the point where the rock entered the water. This often forces that water to spill out over the edges of the puddle.

THE EPICENTER

Tsunamis are usually formed by one of four events: an underwater volcano, a landslide, an earthquake, or the impact of an asteroid. In the case of the 2004 tsunami, the event that created the waves was an enormous underwater earthquake. Geologists specify an epicenter as the point on Earth's surface that is located directly above the earthquake's origin. The epicenter of the December 26, 2004, earthquake was located in the Indian Ocean, less than 60 miles (97 km) off the western coast of the island of Sumatra.

Regular Waves and Tsunami Waves

The biggest difference between normal ocean waves and tsunami waves are their wavelengths. The wavelength is the distance from the crest of one wave to the crest of the next wave. Waves lose energy as they travel. The amount of energy a wave loses depends on its wavelength. Regular ocean waves are created by wind. They have very short wavelengths and lose their energy quickly. A tsunami wave has a very long wavelength and will not lose as much energy as it travels through the ocean. Once these waves reach the shoreline, they still have a great deal of force.

Tectonic Plates

The surface of Earth is a mosaic of about seven large rigid plates, about 60 miles (97 km) thick, called tectonic plates. Basically, these plates are stiff outer layers of rock overlying more ductile rocks deeper in the planet. Tectonic plates are in continuous motion. Their motion is relative to each other due to the slow circulation of Earth's interior as it tries to cool off. On the plate boundaries, rocks are grinding past each other across contact surfaces called faults. Friction on the faults resists sliding as the plates slowly move relative to each other. This causes the rocks next to the fault to deform slightly, storing up energy like a spring. When friction is finally overcome, the rocks on either side of the fault slide to catch up with the overall motion between the plates. This releases the stored energy in an event called an earthquake.

The Andaman-Sumatran Trench

In some regions, called subduction zones, a tectonic plate descends beneath another plate. In the case of the Indian Ocean earthquake, two plates in a subduction zone known as the Andaman-Sumatran trench suddenly shifted. This released

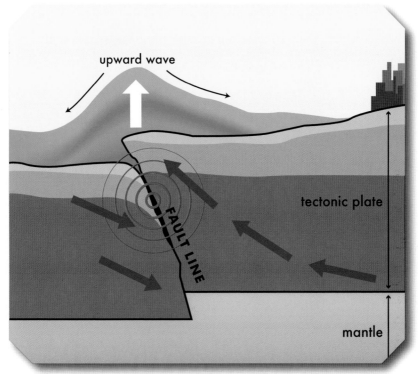

*This diagram shows two tectonic plates pushing against each other.
The released energy causes an earthquake and upward wave.*

more than 250 years of accumulated stored energy.
One plate, the Indian plate, had been shifting north
at approximately 2.5 inches (6.4 cm) a year. It was
gradually sliding under the edge of another plate,
known as the Burma plate. The resulting friction
caused the adjacent rock to deform. When frictional
resistance was suddenly overcome, the slip across
the fault was as much as 50 to 60 feet (15 to 18 m).

Measuring Earthquakes

The Richter scale was developed by Charles F. Richter to classify the size of earthquakes using seismograms (recordings of ground shaking). The scale is based on how much the ground shakes and how far from the source the measurement is made. It indicates the total amount of energy released by the quake. For earthquakes larger than a magnitude 8.0, a different magnitude scale, called the seismic-moment magnitude, is more accurate than the Richter scale. The earthquake responsible for the Indian Ocean tsunami registered a magnitude 9.15 on the seismic-moment magnitude scale, one of the most powerful ever recorded.

The fault area that slipped was about 120 miles (193 km) wide and 800 miles (1,287 km) long, extending to the north from Sumatra and past the Nicobar and Andaman Islands. This is the longest known fault rupture. Located from 3 to 30 miles (5 to 48 km) below the surface of the ocean, the movement of these two plates created a massive earthquake. In terms of the entire planet, it was a very small event. According to geologist Simon Winchester, "The earth shrugged for a moment. Everything moved just a little bit."[1] A geologist would call it only a "seismic bump."

But even if the quake was small in terms of the tectonic shifting of the entire planet, the earthquake measured about 9.15 on the seismic-moment magnitude scale. That measurement indicates a tremendous release of energy. The earthquake was so massive and caused so much rock to suddenly shift that it affected the Earth's rotation. It made the day a few microseconds shorter than normal. It was the third-strongest earthquake in the world since 1900.

THE WAVES

The Indian Ocean tsunami was a direct result of this earthquake. The rock displacements associated with the earthquake caused the ocean bottom to heave up or down, abruptly forcing a huge amount of ocean water to move and create tsunami waves. It is estimated that the earthquake off the coast of Sumatra was large enough to displace trillions of tons of water. This displaced ocean water started to spread out in a series of tsunami waves, expanding away from the 800-mile-(1,287-km-) long earthquake

Other Tsunamis in History

The Asian tsunami of 2004 was not the first tsunami to cause widespread death and destruction. In 1703, a tsunami caused by an earthquake killed more than 100,000 people in Awa, Japan. One of the most devastating volcanic eruptions in history occurred on the island of Krakatoa in Indonesia. In 1883, the island and the seabed around it collapsed and created a tsunami that killed thousands of people. It was felt as far away as England and the West Coast of the United States.

In more recent times, tsunamis hit Hawaii and Alaska in 1946 and again in Alaska in 1964. In May of 1960, an estimated 2,000 people were killed on the coast of Chile when the largest earthquake ever recorded created a tsunami that spread across the Pacific Ocean as far away as Japan. Tsunamis continue to occur, including the one striking the Solomon Islands in the South Pacific on April 2, 2007.

rupture zone. In this zone, the ocean water had suddenly been pushed up (on the western side) or pulled down (on the eastern side) by the underlying rock motions. The biggest tsunami waves moved eastward toward Banda Aceh and Thailand and westward toward Sri Lanka and India.

The spreading tsunami waves pull apart into a series of up-and-down oscillations and travel very quickly in the ocean. In the deep ocean, they travel 500 to 600 miles per hour (805 to 966 km/h), which is about the speed of a passenger jet airplane. Normal ocean waves travel between 35 to 60 miles per hour (56 to 97 km/h). Out on the open ocean, a tsunami wave is hard to detect, as it may be only 2 feet (0.6 m) or less in height, spread out over tens of kilometers on the surface. A boat passing over a tsunami wave will most likely not even notice it.

Once a tsunami wave reaches the shallower ocean near the shore, it begins to drag and slow down. The water behind the wave moves quickly, and as it piles up against the wave, the height of the wave increases. If the ocean floor slopes up to the shore at a steep angle, the tsunami will slow more quickly and pile up faster and higher. A gentler slope from the ocean to the shore slows the waves more gradually so they are

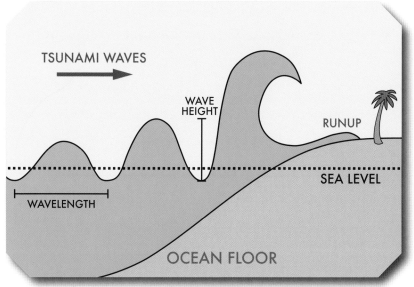

This diagram shows that as wavelengths shorten, wave heights increase, until hitting the coast.

not as high. Tsunami waves may be from 30 to 100 feet (9 to 30 m) high once they finally reach land.

HITTING THE SHORELINE

A tsunami does not affect every shoreline in the same way. The shape of the ocean floor can either increase or decrease a wave's forces. Coral reefs can break up the waves enough to reduce their intensity. Bays and river valleys will suffer greater damage than headlands, because the force of the waves is channeled into a smaller space. If there is a storm

Energy and Water

Tsunami waves are created by the transfer of energy created by an event such as an earthquake. The earthquake may push up on the sea floor as well as an entire column of water. When the water drops back down to sea level, the potential energy from that lifted water (such as in a stretched-out rubber band) is transferred to kinetic energy (such as the rubber band being released). That kinetic energy creates the series of concentric waves that radiate out from the quake and become tsunami waves.

taking place at the same time, the damage of the tsunami's waves will be magnified.

Seismic Waves

The earthquake that occurred in the Indian Ocean also produced seismic P-waves (sound waves) and S-waves (shear waves) that travel through the rock much faster than tsunami waves travel. Within 20 minutes, the P-waves had reached the far side of the world, alerting global seismic monitoring instruments to the occurrence of the great earthquake. The ground in Sri Lanka moved up and down 3.5 inches (9 cm) as the seismic waves passed. This seismic shaking was felt strongly in Sumatra and noticeably around the entire Indian Ocean. But, few people recognized that a disaster of immense proportion was pending. ⌐

A view of the tsunami-stricken areas of Banda Aceh, Indonesia

Barry Hirshom, foreground, and Stuart Weinstein in the Pacific Tsunami Warning Center

A Ripple on the Water

On the afternoon of December 25, 2004, in Hawaii (which in the Indian Ocean would have been December 26), geologists at the Pacific Tsunami Warning Center received alert alarms from two remote seismic monitoring stations.

Barely a minute had elapsed and the computers in Hawaii were picking up the signals. The geologists could tell that a large earthquake had just occurred.

THE PACIFIC TSUNAMI WARNING CENTER

The geologists' first job was to pinpoint the location of the earthquake and issue a warning to as many people as possible that a tsunami could be approaching. Eighteen minutes after the quake, they sent an e-mail bulletin to 26 nations in the Pacific. According to author Geoff Tibballs,

> [They announced] an "event" off the northern coast of Sumatra with a magnitude of 8.0 [on the Richter scale]. However they realized that it was not the centre's Pacific nation clients that needed to be warned. The biggest hit would undoubtedly be in the Indian Ocean but because no warning system existed there, nobody in Honolulu had any indication of whether a tsunami had been generated. In fact, by the time that first bulletin was issued, the tsunami had already hit Banda Aceh on the northern coast of Sumatra.[1]

In that hour, although they had not yet learned about the tsunami, the geologists would receive more data and upgrade the earthquake from an 8.0 to an 8.5 and then to a 9.0. That is ten times greater than the original 8.0 magnitude. Subsequent analysis established the most accurate magnitude as 9.15. This is the third-largest earthquake ever recorded (after the magnitude 9.5 1960 Chile and magnitude 9.2 1964 Alaska earthquakes).

The geologists spent 12 hours on the phone trying to relay the alarm. Geologist Stuart Weinstein remembered,

We spoke to people in the foreign ministries, and everywhere we could think of. ... The message was simple: start walking away from the sea. You just have to be a 15-minute walk away from the sea to be safe.[2]

Unfortunately, it was a holiday for most of the countries in the tsunami's path, and many government officials were not available. Most of the countries and remote island areas also did not have a civil defense warning system. There was no reliable way of passing along the information to the people who were most at risk.

Watches and Warnings

When an earthquake occurs, officials issue tsunami watches or warnings to threatened areas. If an earthquake registers more than 7.0 on the Richter scale, a warning is issued to areas within two hours of tsunami travel time from the earthquake's epicenter. If the earthquake is more than 7.5 in magnitude, the warning is extended to three hours. For locations not in the immediate warning zone, a tsunami watch is issued to areas one hour tsunami travel time beyond the warning zone for a 7.0 quake and three hours tsunami travel time beyond the warning zone for quakes above 7.5.

SUMATRA

Because of the speed at which the tsunami waves traveled and struck land, it is unlikely that even an early warning system could have saved lives in Sumatra. It took only 15 minutes for the first of the tsunami's deadly train of waves to strike. At 65 feet (20 m) in height, the first wave stripped vegetation from the sides of cliffs. Freighters were capsized and smaller boats tossed onto the land.

Creating a Travel Time Map

Stuart Weinstein and his colleagues at the Pacific Tsunami Warning Center pinpointed the epicenter of the earthquake and estimated the speed of the tsunami. They were then able to create a tsunami travel time map. This map gave them an approximate idea of how long it would take for the waves to reach various nations around the Indian Ocean.

It is estimated that tens of thousands of people were killed in those first 15 minutes. The final death toll would approach 200,000 people. A total of seven successive tsunami waves battered the island.

The Sumatran province of Aceh, where Banda Aceh is located, was home to a political separatist movement. The government was attempting to rid the rebels from this area and had not allowed any foreign journalists or aid workers into the province before the tsunami. Consequently, no one was able to accurately report on the damage in the area or help those who were wounded. Remote areas of the island were completely unreachable.

Thailand

Thailand's southwest coast was hit approximately 90 minutes after the earthquake. Because the area was heavily populated with tourist resorts, this was where the highest number of foreigners were killed or reported missing. Approximately half of the reported deaths were foreigners. Many survivors were left without any possessions or documents or any means to contact family or travel home. There were also many children from tourist families who were orphaned as a result of the tsunami.

India

The first tsunami wave struck the coast of India approximately two hours after the earthquake on that Sunday morning. But it was the second and third waves that did the most damage. The Tamil Nadu region was especially hard-hit, with 8,000 deaths. The rushing waters flooded the Madras nuclear power plant, which was constructed to withstand cyclones and tidal waves, and forced an emergency shutdown of the reactor. There was severe property destruction along the coastal areas, where the homes of poor fishermen were destroyed by the waves.

SRI LANKA

The waves reached Sri Lanka at about the same time as India, and because these regions were to the west there was no receding of the ocean and no warning that a tsunami was approaching. Almost 30,000 people were reported dead and another 6,000 were missing. The president of Sri Lanka declared a national disaster, but rescue efforts were slowed because police and military bases had been flooded and communication lines were down. Villagers and rescue workers also faced risks from unexploded land mines, bombs, and shells (remaining from a civil war) that were now exposed by the waves. Even the southwest coast of the country, which geographically should have been protected from

A Tsunami Timeline

The earthquake responsible for the tsunami occurred shortly before 8:00 a.m. local time (in the area of the epicenter) on December 26, 2004. The spread of the waves can be traced by looking at a timeline of when the tsunami hit certain countries in the Indian Ocean over a seven-hour period:

- 15 minutes after the quake: Sumatra
- 30 minutes: Andaman Islands
- 90 minutes: Thailand
- 2 hours: Sri Lanka and India
- 3 hours, 30 minutes: Maldives
- 7 hours: Somalia

One of the tragedies of the tsunami was that many people could have been saved if a warning system had been in place. Most people would have had enough time to reach a safe distance away from the coast had they known the tsunami was approaching.

the waves, was damaged. The waves hit the tip of Sri Lanka and changed direction in a process known as refraction. The shallow water slowed down the front of the wave, but the outer, faster part of the wave curved around the island.

THE MALDIVES AND AFRICA

The Maldives is a cluster of tiny coral islands off the southwest coast of India. They are some of the lowest-lying areas on Earth and received the tsunami's waves almost four hours after the earthquake. Like Thailand, the islands' major industry was tourism, and many resort hotels were devastated. The Maldives are the tips of underwater volcanoes and do not have a continental shelf like large landmasses. This lessened the damage because the tsunami waves just washed through the islands. There were no sloping shelves of land at the coasts to slow the speed of the waves and pile them up, so the tsunami waves did not exceed five feet (1.5 m) in this

Geology and Tsunamis

The power of a tsunami and the effect it has on a land mass can vary depending on the geology of the area. For example, geological features such as coral reefs, bays, the entrance to rivers, and the shape of the seabed can lessen the force of the tsunami's waves. A beach that has a very steep seabed sloping up to it may not receive very much damage because the slope helps to dissipate some of the force of the oncoming water. A beach with a shallow slope, however, will feel the full force of the tsunami waves, and it is more likely that the water will spread inland.

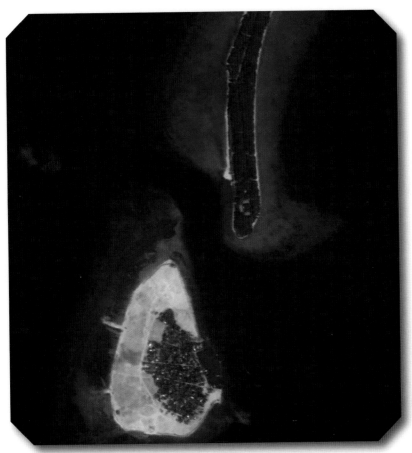

*A satellite photo of the Maldives after being hit
by the tsunami waves*

area. The coral reefs surrounding the islands also
stripped some of the energy from the waves.

The tsunami continued across the Indian Ocean
and hit the coast of Africa about seven hours after
the quake. Death tolls were much lower in this area.

An Eye in the Sky

Two NASA satellites, TOPEX/Poseidon and Jason 1, passed over the tsunami. Both satellites can measure the height of the ocean's surface and detect unusual water levels of 20 inches (51 cm) or more. Because the satellites were not being used for weather detection, the data they collected could not be used to issue a timely warning. However, it was the first time that a tsunami had ever been observed from space.

AFTER THE WAVES

These are just the basic facts about the death and damage that resulted from the 2004 Indian Ocean tsunami. The real story lies in the words of the survivors. Through the eyes of those who lost their families and their homes in the tsunami, the actual situation and scope of the disaster can really be seen. ⌒

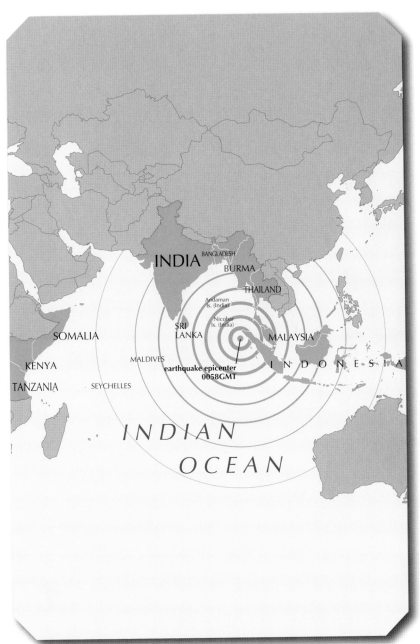

Map of the 2004 Indian Ocean tsunami's impact

*Martin Bleck, of Portugal, near a tsunami warning sign in Thailand
where he was swept away in 2004*

A People-Eating Wave

One of the most vivid and frequently
broadcast video images of the 2004
tsunami is of a peaceful beach resort on Khao Lak,
Thailand. A British tourist took the video from his
hotel room moments before the first wave hit. The

video shows a beautiful sandy beach, palm trees, and the start of another vacation day as workers set up beach chairs. A moment later, an enormous wave appears and washes over the beach toward the hotel.

This is one example of how the waves were viewed from land. The best way to understand the events of the tsunami and how it struck is through the words and images of the survivors.

One of the first and hardest-hit areas was around the city of Banda Aceh in Indonesia. This area not only suffered damage from the tsunami, but from the initial earthquake as well. One survivor described the aftermath of the earthquake,

When [the earthquake] was finished there was a noise like a bomb. Then a gap, then a noise like a ship's engine, and then people started screaming. Everyone started running with the water about thirty meters behind them. Many slipped and fell before they got to high ground. The water simply sucked them away and they disappeared. Everything was destroyed. All the buildings were flattened.[1]

A Desperate Image

One image televised following the tsunami showed a woman running toward the tsunami waves as they struck Krabi Beach in Thailand. Karin Svaerd, a police officer from Sweden, was running to warn her husband and three children of the approaching waves. She was engulfed by the water and swept into a tree. Amazingly, her entire family survived and were found safe just minutes later.

A fisherman named Marwan Saad described his experiences. He lived on a small island off the tip of Sumatra. When the earthquake occurred, he was not too concerned, as this happened frequently in the area. However, about 20 minutes later, the villagers heard what sounded like thunder. Unsure of what they were hearing, the villagers went outside to the beach where they saw the approaching waves. Suddenly, they were running for their lives. Saad recalled,

> The first wave destroyed my house, but the second wave was even bigger. I was submerged up to my neck and the children were completely underwater. I was forced to hold them as best I could. [2]

Saad's family was lucky, however. Even though their home was destroyed, his entire family survived.

Indonesia suffered the most damage from the tsunami, since

Fishing Unawares

Many of the local fishermen in the areas affected by the tsunami were not aware that it had occurred. They had left home early in the morning and taken their boats out to sea as usual, some traveling as far as 12 miles (19 km) away from the shore. There was no indication at sea that anything had happened. But when fishermen returned to their villages in the evening, there was total devastation. Often twice as many women died in these villages as men. The women were either at home or in the fish markets by the sea while the men were safely fishing offshore.

it was closest to the earthquake's epicenter. It is estimated that more than three-quarters of the tsunami deaths took place in Indonesia. A minimum of 800,000 survivors were left homeless and destitute. Despite the terrible odds for the inhabitants of Indonesia, and especially in the Aceh province, there were remarkable stories of survival. One of these stories involved several people who were swept out to sea. They constructed rafts from debris and lived on coconuts and rainwater until they were rescued by passing ships.

Sri Lanka was also heavily damaged by the tsunami. As a result of the wave that swept it from its tracks, the Queen of the Sea would become the worst railroad disaster in history in terms of loss of life. Shenth Ravindra, a British tourist who was on the train, managed to climb off the carriage and onto the roof of a house. He said,

A Town Obliterated

The town of Leupueng in Indonesia was obliterated by the tsunami. Because of its location on the coast, squeezed in between the ocean and coastal limestone cliffs, it had no protection from the tsunami's force. Scientists think that the limestone cliffs may have directed the tsunami's force toward the town, since the waves had nowhere else to go. Nothing was left standing in the town, and only a few hundred residents are thought to have survived.

Visitors look out from the wrecked coach of the Queen of the Sea in Sri Lanka.

I looked back and saw the carriage that had been next to ours floating in the water. The water was choppy and the carriage was being tossed around. I saw a large woman in a pink sari inside the carriage. She was moving back and forth with the momentum of the train. Then I realized it was a dead body.[3]

Ravindra had to wade through the water, which was filled with dead bodies. He gently pushed them to one side until he reached the safety of higher ground.

A cricket team from England's Harrow School was in Galle, Sri Lanka, for a cricket tournament. When the waves came ashore, the team managed to survive by climbing onto the roof of a nearby pavilion. Peter Flach, the father of one of the boys on the team, was on his way to the playing field when the waves stuck. He described his experience,

> *A wall of water picked me up and flung me backwards into the edge of the jungle. I was rolled about underwater like a rag doll. ... I then broke surface and saw the jungle moving past at 30–40 mph. It was dense with a lot of trees and other vegetation. I stupidly tried to grab a palm frond but I was going far too fast and couldn't hold on.*[4]

Flach was finally able to cling to a coconut palm and catch his breath, avoiding oncoming debris such as logs. He eventually let himself be carried by the water to a house, where he was able to climb up and rest.

Michael Dobbs, a reporter for the *Washington Post*, was vacationing in Sri Lanka when the waves hit. He described the scene in the city of Galle when the waves enveloped the city's bus station,

> *Police said at least 200 people were killed at the station, the city's busiest crossroads, as buses were tossed around on the converging cascades of water. Some drowned in their seats;*

some were stabbed by shards of flying glass; some were crushed beneath sheets of metal. By the end of the day, row after row of corpses lay in the baking sun awaiting retrieval.[5]

The waves caused just as much devastation in India. The first wave hit almost an hour before the second and third waves. The latter waves did the most damage. Many religious pilgrims who had journeyed to the Manginapudi beach on the southern coast were swept away when the waves hit. Further south in the Tamil Nadu region, Anton Raj rushed home after hearing of the first wave to see if his parents were safe. Raj said,

My father told me that when the sea level was rising, he and many others actually went to see it! He said it was wonderful to gaze at the rising waters. People say that the sea was not arrogant, just silent. But within minutes, it rose to the height of a two-story building and swept away their homes.[6]

A fisherman in the Indian town of Akkarapettai described his experience,

That morning the sea was like it always is. Then suddenly it was on fire. Boiling. It lifted up 11 yards and paused, almost like it was surveying us below it. And then it fell. It consumed one house after another, like paper boxes.[7]

Warning Signs

Oddly enough, an area that was most vulnerable to the tsunami, India's Andaman and Nicobar islands, had a very high survival rate. These islands are home to six indigenous tribes who live much as their ancestors did. They rub stones together to start fires and hunt and fish using bows and arrows. They have very little contact with the outside world. These tribes usually lived near the sea in leaf and straw huts. However, these tribal people moved to higher ground before the tsunami approached.

Tribal leaders believe that the earth

The Animals Knew

One of the most amazing things about the tsunami is that many animals seemed to have known that the tsunami waves were coming. In Sri Lanka's national wildlife park, despite heavy human losses, no animal corpses were found. Scientists believe that animals have different sensory abilities that enable them to detect earthquake signals that humans require instruments to sense. Some animals can hear tones much lower than those heard by human ears. The underwater earthquake generated low infrasound waves that travel rapidly in the ocean and air; some of these were detected by special acoustic sensors in the Indian Ocean. Animals also sense ground vibration spreading out from an earthquake's epicenter. Mammals, birds, insects, and spiders may feel these waves and have an instinctive flight response. In many cases, they scattered away from the sea. There are stories of elephants breaking free from their ropes and fleeing to higher ground with human passengers and dogs running from the shoreline long before the tsunami waves struck. Humans either cannot sense these vibrations and infrasound or have learned to ignore the sensations.

A Moken man walks on the beach after the village was destroyed on the Surin Islands, Thailand.

communicates with them and warned them of the oncoming waves. According to Ashish Roy, a local environmentalist, the tribes have a connection to nature that has been lost in modern men. The tribes can "smell the wind [and] gauge the depth of the sea with the sound of their oars."[8] Officials believe the tribes escaped the worst of the devastation by paying attention to signs in nature. These included changes in the behavior of marine wildlife and birds—a primitive and age-old early warning system.

Another primitive tribal group, the Moken of Thailand, also had advance warning of the tsunami. According to their tribal chief, stories have been handed down through generations about a "people-eating wave." When the sea receded before the arrival of the first wave, the Moken ran inland.

At a resort on Maikhao Beach in Phuket, a young British girl named Tilly Smith was on the beach with her family the morning of the tsunami. When she saw the sea suddenly retreat from the beach and start to bubble, she remembered learning about the warning signs of a tsunami. Tilly warned her family and the other tourists on the beach. Author Geoff Tiballs wrote about Tilly's warning:

> *"Mummy, we must get off the beach now!" she said. "I think there's going to be a tsunami!" The adults still did not grasp the severity of the situation until she spelled out the magic words: a tidal wave.*

> *[Her warning] spread like wildfire and within seconds the beach was deserted. Her family retreated to the first floor of their hotel and minutes later the water surged right over the beach, demolishing everything in its path. Thanks to Tilly, Maikhao turned out to be one of the few places along the shores of Phuket where nobody was killed.[9]*

In the village of Nam Khem on the coast of Thailand, a woman named Nang was swept up by the wave as she ran inland from her home. She was tumbled and buffeted by the wave of water, unable to surface, until she was thrown against the trunk of a palm tree. Fearing that she would be crushed by oncoming debris, she climbed to the top of the tree. She recalled that,

> *She could see people who had latched onto pieces of wood and refrigerator doors go drifting by. She could hear what sounded like a thousand children calling out for their parents and a thousand parents calling out for their children. Everywhere, people cried out for help. ... All she could see was death.*[10]

The waves subsided, but for those who survived the rushing water, the ordeal was only beginning. The aftermath of the wave would reveal the complete destruction on land.

False Wave Warnings

Four days after the tsunami, on December 30, 2004, the Indian government issued warnings of new tsunamis. Panicked residents fled the coast or climbed onto rooftops as recovery operations were halted. Eventually, the Indian government announced that the warnings were false and there were no new killer waves approaching. They had overreacted to the news of a series of underwater earthquakes recorded near Sumatra. But, these were 1,000 times less powerful than the earthquake that created the tsunami.

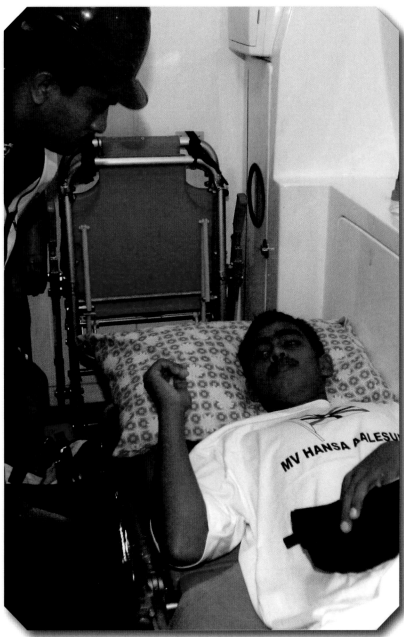

*Tsunami survivor Ari Afrizal after being rescued from a raft
in the Indian Ocean*

Sri Lankans return to the ruins of their home.

The Aftermath

The waves finally receded or settled into stagnant pools, and those who had survived the tsunami were dazed by what had happened in so little time. The ground was littered with rubble and corpses. In many places, not a single structure had survived the onslaught of the waves. As the waters continued to recede, bodies hanging from trees or limbs sticking out of the layers of silt and mud were revealed. In Galle, Sri Lanka, a *Time* magazine reporter interviewed a shopkeeper. The reporter wrote,

> *He walks toward what was once a busy junction in the town and claims that the giant swamp that now obscured the ground hides 500 more corpses. To prove his point, he walks over the marshy landscape of tires, rafters, and mud. "There," he says, pointing to yet another body, lying in the open. "We are standing on bodies right now."[1]*

THE DESTRUCTION

In many cases, the waves had moved far inland, carrying with them cars, trucks, and even large fishing boats. The waves deposited these vehicles on highways or buildings. In the Tamil Nadu area of the Indian coast, an estimated 15,000 fishing boats were destroyed. Reporter Michael Dobbs of the *Washington Post* described the devastation following the tsunami,

> *A day after the disaster, the low-lying coastal road was littered with the debris of wrecked buildings, beached boats, fallen trees and overturned buses and cars. ... The force of*

Waves wash through houses in Sri Lanka.

the water was so great that many of these boats ended up
hundreds of yards inland, crushing the flimsy houses that lay
in their path and killing everyone inside. [2]

As government officials and rescuers flew over the
western coast of Indonesia's Aceh province, they saw
total devastation. Often, only concrete foundation

pads indicated that a large building once stood there. The only signs of smaller homes were scattered and bent corrugated metal roofs. Roads and bridges had been swept away all along the coast, which would make it difficult for rescue and aid workers to enter certain areas.

Bodies were everywhere. Some survivors desperately searched for loved ones. Others, dazed and disoriented as they wandered, were unable to find what was left of their homes. A survivor from the Indonesian village of Leupueng searched the rubble of his parents' house for any signs of his family. He said,

> *I saw eleven bodies there. But I have no idea if they were any of my relatives because their faces have disappeared.*[3]

In the rush to escape the waves, many people found shelter on high ground, often in the jungle. Many had no food or water and spent days sleeping in the open, being bitten by insects. Survivors were injured with

The Statistics

In a situation report issued in February 2005, the World Health Organization (WHO) listed the official numbers of missing and dead from the tsunami disaster. Indonesia experienced the greatest losses with 300 confirmed dead but more than 127,000 people missing and presumed dead. Sri Lanka had almost 31,000 deaths and more than 5,000 people missing. In India, approximately 11,000 people were dead and 5,500 missing. In Thailand, the death toll reached more than 5,000 with more than 3,000 missing. These four countries experienced the most devastating losses of the tsunami disaster.

cuts, bruises, and broken bones from being struck by debris. Tourists and natives alike had taken refuge on the hillsides.

MEDICAL ATTENTION

As the wounded began to trickle into area hospitals, facilities were quickly overwhelmed. Many hospitals in Indonesia were severely understaffed because many medical personnel had died in the tsunami. Soon, makeshift hospitals were set up in any structure that remained standing. The wounded began arriving in greater and greater numbers. Many suffered from deep cuts and scrapes from flying debris, such as trees, shards of glass, and pieces of metal. Others had difficulty breathing because they had inhaled the salty seawater of the tsunami waves. Eventually, these people would begin to suffer from lung infections from the dirty water. Because the

Psychological Scars

WHO has said that nearly all of the people affected by the tsunami will suffer from some psychological trauma. Immediately after the tsunami, many people sat motionless, cried for hours on end, suffered nightmares, or feared anything to do with the ocean. Others abandoned their children or turned to alcohol.

Because so many communities were completely wiped out, people also lost social support systems such as families, prayers, and familiar rituals. Even years after the tsunami, many people still suffer from the loss of homes, families, jobs, and security.

seawater carried raw sewage and other contaminants from the land, even simple cuts and scrapes became infected. Witnesses recalled seeing oil spills, propane, and septic tank refuse in the water.

Soon anyone with any kind of medical or scientific training was pressed into service. Faye Linda Wachs, an American who had been vacationing in Thailand, described how she assisted a group of vacationing nurses and doctors who were helping with the wounded. They were unearthing survivors and carrying them to safety using improvised stretchers made out of doors, box spring mattresses, and bamboo poles. "Apparently the tsunami didn't kill any mosquitoes," Wachs recalled. "We had to keep the wounded covered so they didn't get bites in addition."[4]

Baby 81

Shortly after the tsunami struck Sri Lanka, an unidentified baby was found in the mud and debris and taken to a nearby hospital. He was nicknamed "Baby 81" because he was the eighty-first patient admitted to that hospital. Baby 81 was quickly claimed by nine different couples who had lost babies in the tsunami. Jenita and Murugupillai Jeyarajah insisted that the baby was their son. They rushed into the hospital and attempted to take him, resulting in a brief struggle with the staff. They were forbidden to even pick the baby up. The couple threatened to commit suicide unless the baby was returned to them. Finally, the Jeyarajahs and the baby were taken separately to a clinic for DNA testing paid for by UNICEF. The Jeyarajahs proved to be the baby's parents, and after seven weeks they were reunited with their son.

EMOTIONAL TRAUMA

Survivors suffered from physical trauma, and many would also suffer from emotional trauma. In many cases, they had seen their entire families and their homes swept away in just a moment. As a result, these survivors experienced confusion, depression, and lethargy. Many parents were so devastated by their losses that they left their surviving children alone to fend for themselves. Other parents felt overwhelming guilt because they were unable to save their children. It has been estimated that between one-third and one-half of those killed by the tsunami were children. A survivor described his own family's escape from the waters,

We all ran as fast as we could, but we couldn't get far. I was hanging on to my four-year-old daughter but the force of the water was so great she was ripped from my hands.[5]

Children Alone

Many children, either orphaned by the tsunami or abandoned by parents unable to cope, were left in refugee camps. Often, they could not even give officials their own names. One nine-year-old girl was left to fend for herself in an Indian relief camp. She was not identified until a teacher from her school came to the camp and the little girl ran to her. Of the 330 children who had been in the school, only 50 survived.

Karl Nilsson of Sweden displays a sign asking for help in finding his family after the tsunami in Phuket, Thailand.

The Internet

Technology played a big part in quickly spreading the news of the tsunami disaster to the rest of the world. Tourists staying at broadband- and

Technology and the Tsunami

Many families were separated as a result of the chaos of the tsunami's waters and its ability to sweep people great distances inland. Families posted photographs and notes on the walls of hospitals and other available public spaces, seeking information about missing relatives and friends. The photographs included tourists as well as natives, since many beach resort vacationers were killed or missing.

Technology played a major role in the effort to locate missing persons. Volunteers scanned images of missing persons into a central Internet database, where survivors could look for missing family members—living and dead. This would become increasingly important as time went on, as bodies had to be buried instead of awaiting identification in morgues.

WiFi-enabled hotels could quickly e-mail messages, pictures, and videos back home. Hours after the tsunami struck, blogs on the Internet indicated what had occurred and where to send contributions for tsunami relief. Soon, terrifying images and videos of the tsunami's onslaught were available all over the world.

Slowly, those who survived the tsunami received medical attention. Volunteers and supplies began to arrive. Food, shelter, and clothing became available to those who had lost everything. But, a greater problem threatened the tsunami-stricken region. The hot tropical sun was shining and there were thousands of bodies everywhere.

A tsunami survivor talks on a satellite phone at a station set up by an
international aid organization.

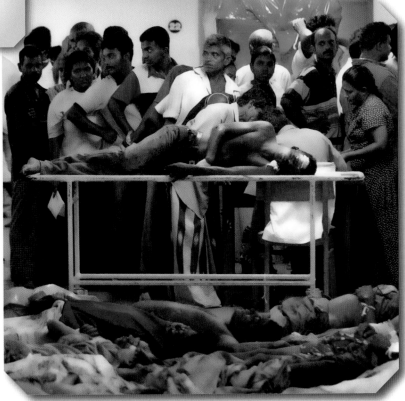

*Victims of the tsunami lie dead next to Sri Lankan civilians lined up to
inquire about missing relatives.*

DEALING WITH THE DEAD

he waves had subsided, but a horrific
scene was left behind. Not only was debris
including homes, boats, buses, and trees strewn
everywhere, but there were also tens of thousands
of bodies. The water had left these bodies hanging

in trees, crushed against walls, and buried under debris and mud. Many were simply lying in streets or floating in rivers and ponds left behind by the floodwaters. Most were naked, since the water had torn the clothing from their bodies. Some bodies looked calm, as if they were asleep. Others were damaged from colliding with debris or being tangled in wires or trees.

Disease

With much of the drinking water contaminated and so many rotting bodies, one of the biggest fears for survivors was disease. Cholera, typhoid, and hepatitis are all diseases that can be spread through drinking unclean water and from having contact with raw sewage.

The Bodies

One tourist in the city of Banda Aceh recalled the scene in the city as she walked down the streets,

> *The cars appeared to be stuck to the walls, alongside the bodies of children and babies. The corpses were bloated and the majority of them had their arms upwards. The smell of the bodies was extremely pungent.*[1]

Decomposing bodies, especially in a hot and humid climate, carry a potential risk of disease. Because of this, it was essential that the dead be dealt with as quickly as possible. However, it was also important that families be able to find and identify their loved ones. At first, bodies were brought to central locations such as temples or community centers and laid out in rows, often hundreds at a time. Officials would separate the bodies of tourists from those of natives, in order to make it easier for people to identify the bodies. A few places had coffins or body bags to place the corpses in, but supplies of these items were quickly exhausted. Most bodies were covered with cloth or plastic sheets.

Collecting the Dead

Collecting the bodies of those killed by the tsunami was one of the most difficult jobs that volunteers and workers faced. Under the unrelenting tropical sunshine, bodies decomposed quickly. Due to the smell and condition of the corpses, workers had to wear masks and gloves. Many workers also wore complete suits of protective clothing in order to protect themselves from contamination or illness.

Sometimes, officials placed dry ice on the bodies to slow the decomposition process. People who had relatives missing searched row by row, looking for a familiar face.

IDENTIFYING THE BODIES

Identifying a body could be difficult after a few days, since many corpses were either damaged beyond recognition or became so bloated that they were unrecognizable. To make matters worse, many of the victims who had died with identification such as wallets in their pockets (especially true for tourists and foreigners) had been looted. Their pockets were slashed and their wallets stolen. Sometimes the only way a family could identify one of its own was by a scrap of clothing still clinging to the body.

With the passage of time, the bodies were in terrible condition and often lost limbs when workers attempted to move them. Families were no longer allowed to view the corpses. Instead, they looked through photographs taken when the bodies were first brought to the makeshift morgues. The photographs had accompanying descriptions of tattoos or other identifying marks, clothing, jewelry, or personal items found with the deceased. Eventually these photographs would be posted on Web sites so that families in other parts of the world could search for their missing relatives. At times, the Web site usage was so high that a site crashed for hours at a time.

At a temple that was turned into a makeshift morgue in Thailand, a doctor and a military official attempted to create an orderly method for processing bodies. Author Erich Krauss described the scene,

> With no time to waste [they] assigned a number to each body and created a folder to correlate with each number. They

The bodies of victims killed by tsunami waves in a mass burial site in India

began with body #1. The doctor worked to determine the cause of death, and [the military colonel] and his men filled out the necessary paperwork. They wrote down a description of the victim's clothing and jewelry and where his body had been found. After taking a fingerprint and photographing the victim, they placed all the paperwork in a folder and moved on to body #2. ... But each time they finished with one batch [of bodies], another batch would come in. By seven o'clock,

*[they] had more than 250 bodies before them. At eight,
more than 300.*[2]

MASS GRAVES

Not every area could deal with the corpses in
this relatively organized manner, however. Some
places had an overwhelming number of corpses. A
mound of more than 200 bodies accumulated under
a bridge on the Kreung Aceh River in Indonesia.
Officials were forced to simply place the bodies
in mass graves and bury them, without attempting
to identify them or record their identities in
photographs or with written descriptions. In other
areas, the deceased were piled together on wagons
and taken to cremation areas. Large fires were lit
with diesel fuel in order to make them burn hotter
and faster. Hundreds of bodies were burned to ash,
with no hopes of ever being identified.

This led to a new trauma for the survivors. Many
survivors experienced psychological damage because
they were unable to see their dead relatives and give
them a proper burial according to the customs of
their culture. Without a grieving process, many
survivors would never fully recover from the losses
they suffered.

Islamic Beliefs

Indonesia is an area where most people practice the Islamic faith. The Islamic teachings require bodies to be buried, not cremated. The deceased must also be carefully washed and wrapped in a white cloth before burial. Burning the bodies or burying them without the proper ceremony made the surviving family members feel as if they had failed to pay proper respect to the dead. Some of the mass graves in Indonesia were estimated to have contained almost 4,000 of these anonymous bodies. Religious authorities finally issued a special fatwa, or decree, relaxing the rules of Islamic burial. The bodies did not need to be wrapped in cloth, and instead of washing each body, a holy man sprinkled water on them before bulldozers covered the bodies with dirt.

Cultural Differences

During the process of trying to identify bodies, cultural differences often clashed when it came to how the dead were being identified. As foreign aid began arriving in the region, experts in identifying bodies also arrived from all over the world. They began processing the dead to create a record for possible future identification. This not only included taking samples of DNA, but also in many cases, performing autopsies to see if there were signs of previous surgeries or injuries that could help to identify the victim. Thai culture does not approve of autopsies. Many Thai officials wanted any bodies that might belong to Thai citizens to be processed with DNA samples only.

DISASTER VICTIM IDENTIFICATION

The task of identifying bodies was overwhelming. Experts in Thailand set up an international group to help in a Disaster Victim Identification (DVI) operation. This operation involved more than 300 investigators from 30 countries. Many of these investigators worked together in the aftermath of wars, natural disasters, and terrorist attacks. Part of the process used by the DVI team was explained by Andrew Marshall in the *Time* magazine article, "How to ID the Bodies." He wrote,

DNA Identification

Forensics experts took samples from the bodies for DNA analysis. The samples were usually in the form of hair, skin, or bone. Once experts received the results, they often implanted a tiny microchip in the body that contained all of its DNA information. Forensic specialists also set up a 24-hour DNA collection point at the airport in Bangkok, Thailand. Relatives could leave their own DNA samples for comparison with any new bodies that arrived at morgues.

Forensic dentists remove teeth or parts of the jaw for lab tests. Biopsies are taken for DNA testing, and fingerprints are lifted. Relatives supply samples of their own DNA in the form of blood and mouth swabs and provide other ... information such as the victims' medical records. Unique marks—moles, scars, tattoos—can also prove decisive in making positive identification. All the data are fed into computers at the DVI Information Management Center in Phuket, which tries to match victims to families. "It isn't rocket science," says [one of the American forensic experts working on the project]. "It's harder than rocket science because it's blended with human emotion."[3]

These international forensic teams also brought supplies and equipment with them to assist in processing the dead.

The Survivors

Slowly, bodies were being processed for identification. But, there were thousands more still missing. Those in need of medical care were being helped, and many of the dead were being dealt with. But many of the physically uninjured were still in desperate need of food, clothing, and shelter in a region that had very few resources. Most had lost their livelihoods and their homes. Who would come to their aid after such a massive catastrophe?

A Thai family member searches through photographs of tsunami victims at a makeshift morgue in Thailand.

*Red Cross trucks loaded with supplies for tsunami victims
in Colombo, Sri Lanka*

HELP ARRIVES

It was not long after the tsunami hit the
Indian Ocean that the world was able
to watch footage of the waves on their televisions.
Tourists in Thailand used e-mail and cell phones to
send eyewitness accounts and pictures almost before

the water had receded. Technology would soon step in to allow people to post pictures of missing loved ones on Web sites. But once the news of the disaster had reached the world, the people directly affected by the tsunami would need more than just the sympathy of their world neighbors. They needed help.

GOVERNMENT AID

Governments and nations around the world were quick to offer relief in the form of money, supplies, and volunteer workers. Just four days after the tsunami struck, United Nations (UN) Secretary General Kofi Annan said that a total of $500 million in aid had been pledged. More pledges soon followed. The largest contribution came from Australia with a pledge of $815 million. Germany followed with $660 million and Japan with $500 million. The United States pledged $350 million in aid. The Emergency Relief Coordinator for the UN, Jan Egeland, said he had "never, ever, seen such an outpouring of

Seeing the Disaster

The disaster affected people in other parts of the world on a personal level because of the many eyewitness photos and videos on the Internet and television. Seeing tourists swept off the beach in video footage taken by people who experienced the disaster created images that could not be easily ignored. Hundreds of thousands of people from all over the world donated money to the tsunami victims.

international assistance in any international disaster, ever."[1]

Humanitarian agencies such as the Red Cross, its counterpart the Red Crescent, and other international groups immediately began rushing aid to the area. A few days after the disaster, pledges had reached a total of $1 billion. People around the world sent donations to the tsunami victims, in amounts as small as five or ten dollars. When former U.S. Presidents Bill Clinton and George H.W. Bush toured the tsunami area as part of their effort to increase aid contributions from private sources, George H.W. Bush said,

> *I don't think there's ever been a tragedy that affected the heartbeat of the American people as much as this tsunami has done.*[2]

According to Michael Elliott in his *Time* magazine article, "Sea of Sorrow,"

Creative Fundraising

In the aftermath of the tsunami, people around the world found creative ways to raise money for the victims. One school painted a permanent mural of a wave on a wall and allowed any student who contributed to their tsunami relief fund the chance to add their painted handprint and name to the mural. A concert held at the Millennium Stadium in Wales raised more than $2 million. A concert held in Los Angeles was broadcast on television. Celebrities such as Madonna, Clint Eastwood, and George Clooney either performed or answered phones as people called in to make pledges.

Volunteers in Sri Lanka carry sacks of donated food.

Like no other disaster in living memory, the Asian tsunami induced a planetary torrent of sorrow, followed by a massive outpouring of money and supplies from public and private sources that at times overwhelmed the relief workers and government agencies trying to deliver water, food, and medicine to those in greatest danger. [3]

Help from Organizations

Many established relief agencies were quick to accept and distribute aid to the tsunami-affected regions. The international aid agency Doctors Without Borders sent 40 workers and 110 tons (98 tonnes) of relief materials. CARE, a charity that aids many countries, delivered food, water-purification tablets, basic medical supplies, and materials for building shelters. The International Rescue Committee airlifted more than 40 tons (36 tonnes) of water-storage tanks and other emergency materials.

Not every attempt at delivering aid went smoothly, however. Deliveries were often delayed because of a lack of organization, damage to infrastructure (such as roads, ports, and airports), and bureaucracy that required donations to pass through customs before being distributed. Badly needed medical supplies sat on airport runways for days waiting to be delivered to devastated areas.

A Princely Job

Britain's Princes William and Harry helped pack tsunami relief kits at a Red Cross warehouse after seeing images of the disaster on television. Prince Harry said that he and his brother had been anxious to become involved.

*U.S. Navy servicemen on board the hospital ship,
the USNS Mercy, off Banda Aceh, Indonesia*

The U.S. Military

The U.S. military played an important role in helping the tsunami-stricken areas. More than two dozen U.S. ships were sent to the region, including the aircraft carrier USS *Abraham Lincoln* and a hospital ship. At the height of the relief effort, more than 16,000 U.S. military personnel were in the area.

They shuttled supplies and rescued survivors with Seahawk helicopters, delivered emergency equipment, and combined with militaries from other countries to create a command center at Thailand's Utapao Air Base.

CIVIL WAR AND AID

Even with this spirit of cooperation, however, the U.S. military encountered uncomfortable situations. Two of the regions affected by the tsunami had been in the midst of civil unrest. Bringing in military aid from other countries was often viewed with suspicion. Sri Lanka had been involved in a civil war since the 1980s. A rebel

Exploited Children

Children were the most vulnerable victims of the tsunami. A dangerous issue came to the attention of relief workers. Many children became victims of criminals who buy and sell children for forced labor or the sex trade. These criminals are called traffickers. With so many children unsupervised after the tsunami, it was easy for the traffickers to abduct them. Messages appeared on the Internet offering these children for sale or adoption. Finally, the Indonesian government banned any child from leaving the country unless the accompanying adults had proof that they were the child's legal parent or guardian. This also prevented well-meaning people from other parts of the world from adopting these orphans. The government felt that children were better off remaining in their own culture, especially after experiencing the trauma of the tsunami and losing their families.

group known as the Tamil Tigers was waging a guerilla war against the Sri Lankan government. The Tamil Tigers were on the U.S. watch list of terrorist groups. After the tsunami, the Tamil Tigers were suspicious of any U.S. military presence in Sri Lanka. The military had to reassure the group that they were in the region only to provide humanitarian aid. They also had to tell the world that bringing this aid to the region did not mean that the United States was supporting the Tamil Tigers.

A similar situation occurred in the Aceh province of Indonesia. The people of Aceh have been fighting for their independence for years. Aceh was one of the regions most damaged by the tsunami, but the Indonesian government restricted the movements of all humanitarian workers in that region. The government claimed that Aceh rebels attacked Indonesian soldiers on humanitarian missions, even though the rebels had declared a cease-fire following the tsunami. The Indonesian government also feared

Internet Donations

In the days following the tsunami, the Internet was the easiest way for individuals to donate money to the relief effort. This was the first major disaster to use the Internet so successfully. Just ten days after the tsunami struck, the Red Cross received $57 million in donations through its Web site. UNICEF received $20 million from online donations, and Oxfam International received 80 percent of its donations online. Doctors Without Borders raised $16 million through Internet donations.

that allowing the U.S. military into the region might lead to the U.S. military assisting the Aceh rebels.

Rescue teams allowed into the region had to deal with looters stealing jewelry from bodies and the accusations that the Indonesian army and police were stealing food aid and selling it in the marketplace. The U.S. Navy helicopter flights that made it into the region were met by mobs of hungry people as they distributed bundles of wheat, protein biscuits, and strawberry yogurt.

As the weeks passed and tsunami aid continued to flow into the area, news coverage of the event subsided. Former President Bill Clinton urged the people of the world to remember their commitment to tsunami relief, saying, "What we have to do now is not to forget these people and places when all the cameras are not there."[4] In the months and years after the tsunami, the world turned its attention to other events. What would become of the people who survived the tsunami and found themselves without homes and jobs?

Tamil Tiger rebel soldiers stand guard in Kilinochchi, Sri Lanka.

A bulldozer clears debris at a resort damaged by the tsunami.

REBUILDING

When the tsunami waves swept across the Indian Ocean, they washed away the homes and means of support for many survivors and their families. Fishermen lost their boats. The destruction of beach resorts that attracted tourists

resulted in a loss of jobs. As Jan Egeland of the UN
commented,

> We cannot fathom the cost of these poor societies and the
> nameless fishermen and fishing villages ... that have just been
> wiped out. Hundreds of thousands of livelihoods have gone.[1]

According to UN statistics, 1 million people
lost their jobs due to the tsunami. This led to a 30
percent unemployment rate in Indonesia. Between
the fishing and tourism industries, Sri Lanka
lost 400,000 jobs in just those few hours of the
tsunami.

Once the immediate needs for medical assistance
and supplies had been met, the countries affected
by the tsunami were in need of long-term aid.
They needed help rebuilding their homes and
infrastructure and help restoring their economies.
These countries feared that once the initial attention
had faded in the tsunami-stricken areas, the world
would forget about them. Even with the $13.6 billion
pledged for humanitarian aid and reconstruction, it
would take years for the local economies to recover.
In January 2005, leaders from seven industrialized
nations (Canada, France, Germany, Italy, Japan, the
United Kingdom, and the United States) announced

that they would temporarily halt any debt repayments owed by countries that had been hit by the tsunami. This would begin to help those countries get back on their feet and be self-reliant, rather than relying on foreign aid for survival.

THE FISHING INDUSTRY

The fishing industry in the area was crippled by the tsunami. Tens of thousands of the traditional wooden boats used for commercial fishing were destroyed. Also damaged were fishing nets, docks, and piers.

The international development agency Action Aid became involved in the construction of a new boatyard in northeastern Sri Lanka. This included teaching local women new job skills such as building new wooden fishing boats.

But it is a slow process to teach people new livelihoods. There were some cases of donated fishing boats being sold for profit or distributed unfairly, rather than finding their way to those impoverished fishermen who needed them most.

Agriculture

The tsunami affected agriculture in the region, which included rice, banana, and mango crops. Seawater flooding contaminated farmland and rice paddies, as well as damaged trees and shellfish spawning areas. It has been estimated that it could take years for agriculture to fully recover.

In the Sri Lankan town of Galle, a local fisherman remarked,

We lost 10 million rupees ($98,000) worth of boats and other material. The government aid of 5,000 rupees ($49) a month obviously was never going to be enough. [2]

Even those who have fishing boats have not been able to recover their standard of living. There are fewer refrigerated trucks to bring the fish catch to markets, so many fishermen simply sell their catch by the side of the highway. In the first few months after the tsunami, many of the usual markets for fish in Japan, Australia, and New Zealand were lost. They feared that any fish caught in the tsunami region had been contaminated by the water, as it contained dirt, debris, and corpses. Some tsunami survivors have been unable to face returning to fishing at all. A former fisherman from Tamil Nadu remarked, "Since my childhood, I've known nothing more closely than the sea. Now I hate it." [3]

Children's Stories

In 2005, a group of children's authors collaborated on a book that tells the stories of 16 children affected by the tsunami. The stories in *Higher Ground* are based on the experiences of these children and explain what it was like when the waves struck. Illustrated with artwork by the survivors, the book shows what the disaster was like from a child's point of view. All money raised by the book went to tsunami relief and rescue funds.

The Tourism Industry

Tourism suffered just as much from the tsunami as the fishing industry, even in places where damage to resort hotels was minimal. In Thailand, Sri Lanka, and the Maldives, tourism plays a major part in their economies. After the tsunami struck, many resorts and restaurants along the ocean were damaged or destroyed. Even those that survived relatively unscathed saw their future guests cancel reservations after seeing the images of death and destruction.

In the Maldives, the damage was estimated at $4.8 billion. According to government spokesman Ahmed Shaheed,

Coral Reefs and Sea Turtles

Scientists feared that many of the area's beautiful and fragile coral reefs had suffered substantial damage because of the tsunami. Many of the shallow coastal regions where coral reefs thrive were hit, as well as mangroves and nesting sites for endangered sea turtles. However, 18 months after the destruction, the news for the coral reefs was positive. Only 13 percent of the coral reefs affected by the tsunami had suffered severe damage, and most of this was due to the earthquake that created the tsunami and not the waves. The reefs that were damaged can be expected to recover in five to ten years. This is good news for the tourism industry.

Sea turtles, however, have not fared as well. Scientists estimated that hundreds of young turtles were dead along the coast, and approximately 20,000 eggs buried in the beach sand were washed away. The damaged or destroyed nesting areas will impact the sea turtle populations for years to come.

The tsunami has within a few minutes set the country back by at least two decades as far as socio-economic development is concerned.[4]

One of the greatest challenges for the industry has been to entice tourists back to these countries.

Experts in the travel industry estimated that it would take three to four years after the tsunami for tourism to recover to previous levels.

VOLUNTEERS

Many volunteers from all over the world have come to the tsunami-stricken regions to help rebuild basic structures, such as homes and schools. Many people who arrived to help rebuild the resort town of Khao Lak in Thailand initially came to the Tsunami Volunteer Center. This center was set up after the tsunami and is involved in many rebuilding projects in the area. In the year following the tsunami, more than 3,500 volunteers from more than 50 countries around the world came to Khao Lak. One young carpenter from Scotland, Aaron Brash, came because he was told that the area was desperate for people with carpentry skills. He said, "I just got into it—there was so much need. People were living in tents all around us: I didn't need much more motivation than that."[5]

REBUILDING CONTINUES

Since the tsunami, progress has been made in rebuilding homes that are stronger and better able to withstand disasters. There has also been progress in restoring livelihoods.

As many countries commemorated the second anniversary of the tsunami, recovery was far from complete. Officials are concerned that aid dollars are not enough for the region to rebuild. Money must also be spent on a warning system to prevent a disaster of this scope from occurring again. But is it possible to put this kind of a system in place?

Marking the Anniversary

The anniversary of the 2004 tsunami is marked with memorial services and other ceremonies of remembrance for those who survived the disaster and those who did not. Survivors light candles on beaches or launch balloons in memory of the dead. Hindu and Buddhist temples ring bells to mark the moment when the first wave struck, followed by moments of silence.

Sri Lankan fishermen try to salvage fishing nets
near a smashed fishing boat.

The first ever DART buoy sits aboard a research vessel in Phuket, Thailand.

LOOKING TO THE FUTURE

On March 28, 2005, a magnitude 8.7 earthquake struck just east of the 2004 rupture zone, and it caused many deaths from the local tsunami. This was the second largest event of the past 40 years. Seismologists are worried about

more great earthquakes happening along eastern
Sumatra, where there have been magnitude 8.5–9.0
events in the past.

On April 2, 2007, a magnitude 8.0 earthquake
occurred beneath the ocean in the South Pacific,
east of Australia, when the Australian tectonic plate
suddenly slid beneath the Pacific plate. Moments
later, a tsunami crashed upon the shores of the
Solomon Islands, destroying entire villages and
sending waves up to a half-mile
(.8 km) inland. "We ran for our lives,
away from the waves," one resident
said. "When we looked back, we saw
our house being destroyed."[1] More
than 20 people were killed, and
the earthquake triggered tsunami
warnings for Australia and even as far
off as Hawaii.

While these tsunamis were not
as devastating as the 2004 Indian
Ocean tsunami, they were sobering
reminders that tsunamis are difficult
to predict and can strike at any time.
While scientists work hard to predict
tsunamis and establish a workable

**The Warning Signs
of a Tsunami**

It is possible to survive a
tsunami by remembering
three basic warning signs:
1. If the ground shakes
near a beach, it could be
the result of an earthquake
and a tsunami may be
coming. Move to higher
ground.
2. If the ocean suddenly
pulls away from the shore,
exposing the seabed, do
not stop to look.
3. Tsunamis are made up
of more than one wave,
and these waves may be
an hour apart. Do not
return to the beach until
an official announcement
declares it is safe.

early warning system, there is only so much that can be done. Many parts of the world remain vulnerable to a tsunami's destruction.

The Ring of Fire

The Ring of Fire, formally known as the circum-Pacific seismic belt, is a horseshoe-shaped zone that partially surrounds the basin area of the Pacific Ocean. It stretches from Australia, up the Asian coast, and around to Alaska and the West Coast of the United States, then down to South America. It is an almost continuous series of ocean trenches and volcanoes associated with major plate boundaries. Motions between the plates occur along thousands of miles of faults ringing the Pacific Ocean, producing 90 percent of the world's earthquakes and 81 percent of its largest events. Volcanoes occur above subduction zones where plates descend below other plate margins, producing the Ring of Fire. As a result, most of the world's tsunamis occur in this region.

THE RING OF FIRE

The Pacific Ocean, with the greatest risk of tsunamis, has had an early warning system in place since 1949. Many subduction zones lie in the Pacific. This results in a large number of active volcanoes and earthquakes. As a result, the region is known as the Ring of Fire. It is home to more than half of the world's volcanoes and almost all of the world's major earthquakes. All seismic activity in the region is monitored from two locations in the United States: the Pacific Tsunami Warning Center (PTWC) in Hawaii and the West Coast/Alaska Tsunami Warning Center (WCATWC) in Alaska. When a large earthquake is detected at global networks of seismic

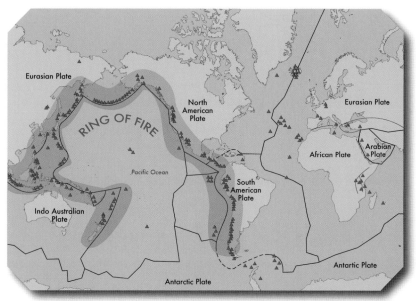

Map of the ring of subduction zones in the Pacific Ocean known as the Ring of Fire

stations, the event is located and its size is estimated. These warning centers then send bulletins to the 27 countries that belong to the International Tsunami Warning System for the Pacific Ocean. The centers try to assess whether the earthquake had a location, depth, faulting geometry, and enough deformation to set off a tsunami. Then, using computer-generated simulations, they determine the possible path of that tsunami.

TSUNAMI DETECTION

Once an earthquake has occurred, the potential
for a tsunami can be evaluated using several
methods. Seismic sensors detect signals from the
initial earthquake or volcanic activity that might
spawn a tsunami. But since not every occurrence will
result in a tsunami, scientists also need methods for
directly detecting actual tsunami waves. Scientists
rely on sea-based instruments for this. Pressure
recorders in the deep ocean measure the weight
of the water above them, which varies according to the
height of the waves. These pressure sensors can detect
a tsunami wave only 0.5 inch (1.27 cm) high.

A Matter of Time

Most scientists agree that it is only a matter
of time before the next destructive tsunami
strikes. Researchers studying the Canary
Islands, in the Atlantic Ocean off the coast of
Africa, are monitoring the Cumbre Vieja
volcano on the island of La Palma. If the volcano erupts, it could send a large chunk of land
into the sea. This could spawn a tsunami with
the potential to submerge the Atlantic coast
of the United States with waves more than 30
feet (9 m) high. This would affect cities such as
Boston, New York, and Miami. In the Pacific,
scientists are studying Anak Krakatoa, a new
volcano that is growing on the site of the first
Krakatoa. When the 1883 volcano erupted, it
triggered a tsunami that drowned more than
37,000 people on the islands of Java and Sumatra. Volcanoes located in Hawaii are some
of the most active in the world. They are a
cause for concern because landslides on the
margins of the islands could create tsunamis
that would devastate Hawaii, California, Japan,
and Australia.

This information is relayed to a buoy on the ocean's surface, which measures surface conditions and relays that information via satellite to ground stations. Scientists also use tide gauges to measure the sea level at the coast and determine whether it is rising or falling. This tsunami monitoring system is known as the Deep-ocean Assessment and Reporting of Tsunamis (DART) system. The DART system is capable of detecting tsunamis when they are still far out to sea, providing more time to warn countries in regions that will be affected.

Another system, known as the Global Sea Level Observing System (GLOSS) uses tidal gauges placed on land, either on the coast of a mainland or on islands out at sea. These gauges monitor the sea level and alert scientists if it is rising at an unnatural rate.

INDIAN OCEAN BUOY

When the 2004 Indian Ocean tsunami struck, the only warning most people had was the sight of

GLOSS Stations

Before the 2004 tsunami, there were 70 GLOSS gauge stations in the Indian Ocean. However, they were only used to measure sea level for long-term climate change studies and only transmitted data occasionally. Now, these GLOSS stations are being updated to transmit data via satellite to new tsunami centers. The stations are being fitted with solar panels to keep them operational even when their main power supply is interrupted by severe weather.

a gigantic wave bearing down on them. The Indian Ocean nations had no tsunami alerting system in place. Even if they had, there was no reliable infrastructure for getting this information to people quickly. Since the tsunami, countries in the region have been working to install a warning system similar to that in the Pacific Ocean. In December 2006, the first buoy for an Indian Ocean DART system was placed 620 miles (998 km) off the coast of Thailand near the Nicobar Islands. The cost of the buoy was shared between the United States and Thailand. The U.S. ambassador to Thailand, Ralph Boyce, remarked,

> With the launching of this buoy, we are taking a big step forwards in better protecting hundreds of millions of people living across the Indian Ocean. [2]

This is the first buoy in what is hoped will be a network of 24 buoys extending to Indonesia and Australia along an unstable fault line. The countries vulnerable to a potential tsunami will have to install warning sirens to alert their population. As of yet, there are not many of these sirens.

OTHER DEFENSES

The Japanese government has invested billions of dollars in constructing coastal defenses such as concrete sea walls and gates that slam shut to protect harbors. Some regions prone to tsunamis prepare for potential disasters with hazard-mapping computer programs. These programs simulate the effect of tsunami waves on a digital representation of an area of coastline. This helps planners predict when a tsunami wave would hit the coast, how high it would be, and how far inland it would reach. This also aids in planning evacuation routes and keeps major municipal buildings, such as hospitals, from being constructed in zones that might be flooded as a result of a tsunami.

PLANNING FOR THE FUTURE

Researchers at the O.H. Hinsdale Wave Research Laboratory at Oregon State University use a wave simulation tank to create miniature tsunami waves and study their effects on coasts

Collecting Evidence

Immediately after a tsunami strikes, teams of scientists collect evidence to help them study and learn from the event. They measure watermarks on buildings and the height of debris left in trees and on roofs. These scientists make note of plants and trees killed by the seawater, as well as where debris and beach sand have been deposited inland. Also noted are the shape and location of erosion on the shoreline. Scientists also speak with survivors and eyewitnesses. All of this evidence helps them create a picture of the tsunami and its force and movement.

and structures. Researchers also want to educate the public about the threat of tsunamis and what should be done when a warning is given. Disaster planners need to create a realistic evacuation plan in the event of an approaching tsunami.

For those who lived through the 2004 Indian Ocean tsunami, it will take many years for life to return to normal. Even with homes and businesses rebuilt and jobs returning to the area, there will always be a lingering fear of when the next unexpected tsunami will strike.

A man watches the sunset at Lampuuk in Indonesia in 2005.

TIMELINE

1883	1949	2004
A major earthquake on the island of Krakatoa, Indonesia, generates a tsunami that kills more than 36,000 people.	An early warning system for tsunamis is installed in the Pacific Ocean.	On December 26, at 7:59 a.m, an earthquake occurs on the ocean floor off the coast of Sumatra in Indonesia.

2004	2004	2004
On December 26, a second tsunami warning is issued.	On December 26, at 9:30 a.m., tsunami waves begin striking the coasts of Sri Lanka, India, and Thailand.	On December 26, at 11:30 a.m., tsunami waves strike the Maldives.

2004

On December 26, seismic signals from the quake trigger an alert at the Pacific Tsunami Warning Center in Honolulu, Hawaii.

2004

On December 26, the first warnings are issued about possible tsunamis.

2004

On December 26, at 8:15 a.m., the first tsunami waves strike the coast of northern Sumatra and then the Andaman Islands.

2004

On December 26, at 3:00 p.m., tsunami waves start to impact the east coast of Africa.

2004

On December 27, the world realizes the enormous scale of the tsunami disaster. Survivors search for family members using the Internet.

2004

Relief operations get underway on December 28 to aid the tsunami victims. Rescue and aid teams arrive in the Aceh province of Sumatra.

TIMELINE

2004	2004	2005
On December 30, the Indian government warns of a possible new tsunami wave.	As of December 31, 6,000 people missing in Thailand are presumed dead.	On January 2, the United Nations predicts that tsunami deaths will reach 150,000. Later reports indicate that 250,000 are dead or missing.

2005	2005	2005
The civil war in Aceh ends in August. It is now easier for foreign volunteers to aid in rebuilding and relief efforts.	A group of authors collaborate on a book telling stories of 16 children affected by the tsunami. Profits go to relief funds.	December 26 marks the one-year anniversary of the tsunami. Many people are still without homes and livelihoods.

2005

2005

2005

Americans are asked on January 3 to donate to tsunami relief efforts.

The WHO issues a report in February that lists numbers of the missing and dead.

Another great earthquake strikes Sumatra on March 28. Local tsunamis take thousands of lives.

2006

2006

2007

In April, civil war escalates in Sri Lanka, interfering with rebuilding efforts.

The first buoy for the Indian Ocean DART system is placed off the coast of Sumatra on December 1.

A tsunami strikes the Solomon Islands west of Australia on April 2.

ESSENTIAL FACTS

DATE OF EVENT

December 26, 2004

PLACE OF EVENT

The Indian Ocean, Thailand, Indonesia, Sumatra, Maldives, India, Sri Lanka, and the east coast of Africa

KEY PLAYERS

❖ Victims and survivors of the tsunami

❖ Volunteers

❖ The people around the world who made donations to the recovery effort

❖ Pacific Tsunami Warning Center

❖ The United Nations

❖ Former presidents Bill Clinton and George H.W. Bush

❖ Doctors Without Borders

❖ CARE

❖ The International Rescue Committee

❖ The U.S. military

❖ Countries that offered aid, including: Australia, Canada, France, Germany, Italy, Japan, United Kingdom, and the United States

Highlights of Event

❖ An earthquake occurred beneath the Indian Ocean on December 26, 2004.

❖ The earthquake generated a tsunami. In the seven hours following the quake, the populations of more than five countries were devastated.

❖ Following the tsunami, relief supplies, aid, and volunteers poured in from all over the world to assist the victims.

❖ The final death toll, although it will never be exact, may be as high as 250,000 people.

❖ Several years after the tsunami, reconstruction was not complete and many people were still without homes and the means for making a living. Officials feel that many lives could have been saved if people had advanced warning of the tsunami. An early warning system similar to that in the Pacific Ocean is being constructed in the Indian Ocean.

Quote

"We cannot fathom the cost of these poor societies and the nameless fishermen and fishing villages ... that have just been wiped out. Hundreds of thousands of livelihoods have gone."
—*Jan Egeland, head of the United Nations Office for the Coordination of Humanitarian Affairs*

ADDITIONAL RESOURCES

SELECT BIBLIOGRAPHY

Krauss, Erich. *Wave of Destruction: The Stories of Four Families and History's Deadliest Tsunami.* Emmaus, PA: Rodale Press, 2006.

Morris, Ann, and Heidi Larson. *Tsunami: Helping Each Other.* Minneapolis, MN: Millbrook Press, 2005.

Stewart, Gail B. *Catastrophe in Southern Asia: The Tsunami of 2004.* Farmington Hills, MI: Lucent Books, 2005.

Tibballs, Geoff. *Tsunami: The World's Most Terrifying Natural Disaster.* London: Carlton Books, 2005.

Walker, Niki. *Tsunami Alert!* New York: Crabtree Publishing Company, 2006.

FURTHER READING

Fredericks, Anthony. *Tsunami Man: Learning About Killer Waves with Walter Dudley.* Hawaii: University of Hawaii Press, 2002.

Kehret, Peg. *Escaping the Giant Wave.* New York: Simon & Schuster, 2000.

Morpurgo, Michael. *Higher Ground.* London: Chrysalis Children's Books, 2005.

Prager, Ellen J. *Furious Earth: The Science and Nature of Earthquakes, Volcanoes, and Tsunamis.* New York: McGraw-Hill, 2000.

Thompson, Luke. *Natural Disasters: Tsunamis.* New York: Children's Press, 2000.

Web Links

To learn more about the 2004 Indian Ocean tsunami, visit ABDO Publishing Company on the World Wide Web at **www.abdopublishing.com**. Web sites about the 2004 Indian Ocean tsunami are featured on our Book Links page. These links are routinely monitored and updated to provide the most current information available.

Places To Visit

O.H. Hinsdale Wave Research Laboratory
Oregon State University
3550 SW Jefferson Way, Corvallis, OR 97331
541-737-3631
wave.oregonstate.edu
This laboratory is a center for research and education about coastal engineering and shoreline science. Teachers can request tours for K-12 students at the laboratory.

Pacific Tsunami Museum
130 Kamehameha Avenue, Hilo, HI 96720
808-935-0926
www.tsunami.org
This museum educates the public about tsunamis in Hawaii and the Pacific region. It has exhibits, programs, and holds events related to tsunami education.

Pacific Tsunami Warning Center
U.S. Dept. of Commerce/NOAA/NWS
1-270 Fort Weaver Road, Ewa Beach, HI 96706
808-689-8207
www.prh.noaa.gov/ptwc
This center monitors the risk of tsunamis and issues warnings in the Pacific Ocean. It is the interim monitoring center for the Indian Ocean. Tours can be scheduled to view the center.

Glossary

asteroid
A small rocky body that orbits the sun.

catastrophe
A sudden and widespread disaster.

concentric
Rings or circles that have the same center point.

contaminant
Something unclean or hazardous that makes something else unusable or spoiled.

cricket
A game popular in England, played with bats, balls, and wickets.

ductile
Able to be twisted or bent, having an alterable shape.

forensic
Type of science that answers questions important to the legal system.

headlands
A cliff or a high area of land that juts into a large body of water.

indigenous
Originating in or characteristic of a particular place or country.

infrasound
A sound with frequencies below the usual range of human hearing.

infrastructure
The basic facilities and systems of a country or a city, such as transportation, communication, and schools.

magnitude
> The size, amount, or strength of something such as an earthquake.

rice paddies
> Fields where rice is grown.

seismic
> Caused by an earthquake or a vibration of the earth.

separatist
> A person or a group that wants to separate or withdraw from an existing government.

stagnant
> Air or water that is not flowing or moving.

subduction
> The process in which the earth's tectonic plates collide and are drawn beneath each other.

tectonic
> Having to do with the structure of the earth's crust.

trafficker
> Someone who conducts illegal trade in things such as drugs or human beings.

tremors
> Movements or vibrations following an earthquake.

Source Notes

Chapter 1. Swept Away
1. Alan Morison. "Phuket Paradise Washed Away." *CNN*. 26 Dec. 2004. <http://www.cnn.com/2004/WORLD/asiapcf/12/26/phuket.eyewitness/>.
2. Erich Krauss. *Wave of Destruction: The Stories of Four Families and History's Deadliest Tsunami.* Emmaus, PA: Rodale Press, 2006. 87.
3. "Eyewitnesses Recount Tsunami Terror." *CNN*. 23 June 2005. <http://www.cnn.com/2004/WORLD/asiapcf/12/26/asia.quake.eyewitness/>.
4. Simon Elegant. "A City of Debris and Corpses." *Time*. 2 Jan. 2005. <http://www.time.com/time/magazine/article/0,9171,1013249,00.html>.

Chapter 2. A Seismic Bump
1. Evan Thomas and George Wehrfritz. "Tide of Grief." *Newsweek*. 10 Jan. 2005. <http://www.newsweek.com/id/48156>.

Chapter 3. A Ripple on the Water
1. Geoff Tibballs. *Tsunami: The World's Most Terrifying Natural Disaster.* London: Carlton Books, 2005. 21.
2. Ibid. 23.

Chapter 4. A People-Eating Wave

1. Geoff Tibballs. *Tsunami: The World's Most Terrifying Natural Disaster*. London: Carlton Books, 2005. 35.
2. Ibid. 37.
3. Ibid. 46–47.
4. Peter Flach. "December 26, 2004 Tsunami Experience." *Belmont Lounge* blog. 31 Dec. 2004. <http://belmontlounge.blogspot.com>.
5. Michael Dobbs. "What I Saw: A Reporter's Account of Tsunami." *Washington Post*. 28 Dec. 2004. <www.newsday.com/news/nationworld/nywosril228,0,6286886,print.story>.
6. Geoff Tibballs. *Tsunami: The World's Most Terrifying Natural Disaster*. London: Carlton Books, 2005. 70.
7. Michael Elliott. "Sea of Sorrow." *Time*. 2 Jan. 2005. <http://www.time.com/time/magazine/article/0,9171,1013255,00.html>.
8. B.S. Kakkilaya. "Asian Tsunami: Lessons from the Survivors." *Nature Sync*. 17 Mar. 2007 <http:// www.naturesync.org/tsunami1.htm>.
9. Geoff Tibballs. *Tsunami: The World's Most Terrifying Natural Disaster*. London: Carlton Books, 2005. 76–77.
10. Erich Krauss. *Wave of Destruction: The Stories of Four Families and History's Deadliest Tsunami*. Emmaus, PA: Rodale Press, 2006. 114–115.

Chapter 5. The Aftermath

1. Michael Elliott. "Sea of Sorrow." *Time*. 2 Jan. 2005. <http://www.time.com/time/magazine/article/0,9171,1013255,00.html>.
2. Michael Dobbs. "What I Saw: A Reporter's Account of Tsunami." *Washington Post*. 28 Dec. 2004. <www.newsday.com/news/nationworld/nywosril228,0,6286886,print.story>.
3. Geoff Tibballs. *Tsunami: The World's Most Terrifying Natural Disaster*. London: Carlton Books, 2005. 34.
4. Joe Eskenazi. "Holiday Turned Nightmare for Berkeley grad." *J. The Jewish News Weekly of Northern California*. 7 Jan. 2005. <http://www.jewishsf.com>.
5. Geoff Tibballs. *Tsunami: The World's Most Terrifying Natural Disaster*. London: Carlton Books, 2005. 34.

Source Notes continued

Chapter 6. Dealing with the Dead
1. Geoff Tibballs. *Tsunami: The World's Most Terrifying Natural Disaster.* London: Carlton Books, 2005. 30.
2. Erich Krauss. *Wave of Destruction: The Stories of Four Families and History's Deadliest Tsunami.* Emmaus, PA: Rodale Press, 2006. 166.
3. Andrew Marshall. "How to ID the Bodies." *Time.* 10 Jan. 2005. <http://www.time.com/time/magazine/article/0,9171,1015889,00. html>.

Chapter 7. Help Arrives
1. Michael Elliott. "Sea of Sorrow." *Time.* 2 Jan. 2005. <http://www.time.com/time/magazine/article/0,9171,1013255,00.html>.
2. "Ex-Presidents: Don't Forget Commitment to Tsunami Relief." *CNN.* 19 Feb. 2005. <http://www.cnn.com/2005/WORLD/asiapcf/02/19/tsunami.bush.clinton/index.html>.
3. Michael Elliott, "Sea of Sorrow." *Time.* 2 Jan. 2005. <http://www.time.com/time/magazine/article/0,9171,1013255,00.html>.
4. "Ex-Presidents: Don't Forget Commitment to Tsunami Relief." *CNN.* 19 Feb. 2005. <http://www.cnn.com/2005/WORLD/asiapcf/02/19/tsunami.bush.clinton/index.html>.

Chapter 8. Rebuilding
1. Seth Mydans. "Toll in Undersea Earthquake Passes 25,000; A Third of the Dead Are Said to Be Children." *The New York Times*. 28 Dec. 2004. <http://www.nytimes.com/2004/12/28/international/asia/28quake.html?_r=2&ex=1188964800&en=191478ed3da62355&ei=5070&oref=slogin&oref=slogin>.
2. Sanjoy Majumder. "Tsunami Fishermen Struggle to Cope." *BBC News*. 30 Dec. 2005. <http://news.bbc.co.uk/2/hi/south_asia/4534868.stm>.
3. Michael Elliott. "Sea of Sorrow." *Time*. 2 Jan. 2005. <http://www.time.com/time/magazine/article/0,9171,1013255,00.html>.
4. Geoff Tibballs. *Tsunami: The World's Most Terrifying Natural Disaster*. London: Carlton Books, 2005. 116.
5. Kate McGeown. "Helping Tsunami-Hit Thailand Rebuild." *BBC News*. 20 Dec. 2005. <http://news.bbc.co.uk/2/hi/asia-pacific/4545614.stm>.

Chapter 9. Looking to the Future
1. "Tsunami Strikes Solomon Islands." *BBC News*. 2 Apr. 2007 <http://news.bbc.co.uk/2/hi/asia-pacific/6516759.stm>.
2. "Tsunami Buoy Laid in Indian Ocean. " *BBC News*. 1 Dec. 2006. <http://news.bbc.co.uk/1/hi/world/south_asia/6197766.stm>.

Index

ABOUT THE AUTHOR

Marcia Amidon Lusted has written ten nonfiction books for children, as well as many magazine articles. She is also a writing instructor and a musician. She lives in New Hampshire with her husband and three sons.

PHOTO CREDITS